Lerner SPORTS

T0015625

...ESPORTS...
SUPERSTARS

Marie-Therese Miller

Lerner Publications ◆ Minneapolis

SPORTS THRILLS
MEET
RESEARCH SKILLS

Lerner SPORTS

Free Database Trial: **lernersports.com**

To John Vincent, the esports superstar of the Miller clan

Copyright © 2024 by Lerner Publishing Group, Inc.

All rights reserved. International copyright secured. No part of this book may be reproduced, stored in a retrieval system, or transmitted in any form or by any means—electronic, mechanical, photocopying, recording, or otherwise—without the prior written permission of Lerner Publishing Group, Inc., except for the inclusion of brief quotations in an acknowledged review.

Lerner Publications Company
An imprint of Lerner Publishing Group, Inc.
241 First Avenue North
Minneapolis, MN 55401 USA

For reading levels and more information, look up this title at www.lernerbooks.com.

Main body text set in Aptifer Sans LT Pro. Typeface provided by Linotype AG.

Designer: Viet Chu
Lerner team: Martha Kranes

Library of Congress Cataloging-in-Publication Data

Names: Miller, Marie-Therese, author.
Title: Esports superstars / Marie-Therese Miller.
Description: Minneapolis, MN : Lerner Publications, [2024] | Series: Learner sports. Esports zone | Includes bibliographical references and index. | Audience: Ages 7–11 | Audience: Grades 4–6 | Summary: "As more people watch and play esports, people from around the world have become famous for their gaming abilities. Meet amateur and professional gamers and learn how they started their esports careers"— Provided by publisher.
Identifiers: LCCN 2022046153 (print) | LCCN 2022046154 (ebook) | ISBN 9798765602928 (paperback) | ISBN 9781728490892 (library binding) | ISBN 9781728497464 (ebook)
Subjects: LCSH: eSports (Contests)—Juvenile literature. | Video gamers—Biography—Juvenile literature. | BISAC: JUVENILE NONFICTION / Biography & Autobiography / Sports & Recreation
Classification: LCC GV1469.34.E86 M55 2024 (print) | LCC GV1469.34.E86 (ebook) | DDC 794.8—dc23/eng/20221013

LC record available at https://lccn.loc.gov/2022046153
LC ebook record available at https://lccn.loc.gov/2022046154

Manufactured in the United States of America
1-53020-51038-2/21/2023

TABLE OF CONTENTS

FORTNITE WORLD CUP

THOUSANDS OF FANS CHEER AS THEY WATCH THE 2019 *FORTNITE* WORLD CUP. Arthur Ashe Stadium is sold out and full of noise. Sixteen-year-old Kyle "Bugha" Giersdorf from Pottsgrove, Pennsylvania, sits onstage in front of a computer screen and a camera. Fans watch the action on hundreds of screens.

Giersdorf focuses as more players are cut from the game. He hardly notices the cheering fans as he knocks out other gamers. The match comes down to Giersdorf and one other player. With one amazing final shot, Giersdorf wins the competition. He wins a whopping three million dollars!

Fast Facts

- Bruce Baumgart won the first esports competition at Stanford University in California in 1972.

- *Fortnite* player Benjy David Fish was only fifteen years old when he signed his first pro contract.

- Xiaomeng Li became the first woman to win the Hearthstone Grandmasters Global Finals in 2019.

- In 2016, the University of California, Irvine (UCI), became the first US public university to have an official esports team.

CHAPTER 1
WHAT ARE ESPORTS?

ESPORTS ARE VIDEO GAME COMPETITIONS ON COMPUTERS OR CONSOLES. Single players or teams compete in tournaments to get the top position. Sometimes they win a big cash prize!

Pro esports athletes earn money by competing in tournaments. These players usually sign with pro teams, such as NRG and 100 Thieves. The teams pay the players a salary. Many teams have coaches, arenas, and gaming gear such as powerful computers to support their players.

Vivian "roxi" Schilling plays *Valorant* on the team Guild X.

Amateur esports athletes do not receive salaries to play games. Amateur competitions offer less money in prizes. College esports players also don't receive salaries, but they can earn college scholarships to help pay for school. They play in school competitions against other college athletes. Sometimes they also play in other amateur events.

Fans at an esports event gather to watch a *League of Legends* tournament.

Defense of the Ancients 2 is a popular multiplayer online battle arena game.

Types of Games

Esports players compete in many kinds of video games. Multiplayer online battle arena (MOBA) games include titles such as *League of Legends* and *Defense of the Ancients 2*. In MOBA games, each team tries to capture the other team's base.

First-person games are popular with esports players around the world.

Players in many first-person games try to destroy or capture players on opposing teams. First-person games are played from the character's point of view. The first-person point of view helps players feel as if they are part of the action.

THE *HEARTHSTONE* CHAMP

Xiaomeng "Liooon" Li is a pro esports player from China who plays *Hearthstone*. Li was the first woman to win the Hearthstone Grandmasters Global Finals. She took the top prize of $200,000 at BlizzConn 2019. Li encourages girls and women to get involved with esports.

In real-time strategy games, players have an overhead view. They try to build resources and take territory. Sports games are based on physical sports, such as football. Soccer, basketball, and hockey also have popular video game titles. Collectible card games are played with virtual cards. *Virtual* means "existing online or on a computer." *Hearthstone* is a virtual card game.

Some esports games, such as *Hearthstone*, can be played on mobile devices.

CHAPTER 2

PRO ESPORTS SUPERSTARS

STANFORD UNIVERSITY IN CALIFORNIA HOSTED THE FIRST ESPORTS COMPETITION IN 1972. Twenty players competed in *Spacewar!* Bruce Baumgart won the free-for-all competition. The prize was a free year of *Rolling Stone* magazine. He was

At esports events, gamers use the same gear to ensure that no one has an advantage.

the first esports champion ever. The esports industry has grown a lot since 1972. Esports players can now win millions of dollars in prizes at competitions.

The road to becoming a pro esports player is different for everyone. Most esports pros start with a passion for a game. They practice for hours to improve their skills. They watch games to learn strategies and fix their mistakes. They stay healthy by exercising. They also make sure to eat and sleep well.

Benjy David Fish

Benjy "benjyfishy" David Fish was only fifteen years old when he joined pro esports company NRG. He competed in the *Fortnite* 2019 World Cup at the age of sixteen. He teamed up with Martin "MrSavage" Foss Andersen in 2021 to win the Europe DreamHack Open Finals. Fish has earned over half a million dollars at *Fortnite* tournaments.

Benjy "benjyfishy" David Fish has nearly four million followers on Twitch.

Fish uses his esports experience to teach others how to master games such as *Fortnite*.

Fish was born April 2, 2004. He was only eight months old when his dad died from cancer. He grew up with his mom and brother in England. Fish competed in bowling events. He also played rugby and cricket. But when his knees started hurting, his doctor told him to take a break from physical sports. He turned to gaming.

Fish started by playing *Wii Sports Bowling* with his brother. He began playing other games such as *League of Legends* when he was eight. He started playing *Fortnite* at thirteen.

Over 300 million people around the world have played *Fortnite*.

Valorant players compete for big prizes, such as the Valorant Champions Tour's $300,000 top prize.

Fish practiced *Fortnite* eight to ten hours each day for competitions. He played in scrimmages and tournaments. He streamed his games on Twitch and YouTube. Fish watched his old games to learn how to play better. He traveled all over the world playing in *Fortnite* tournaments. In 2022, he switched to the game *Valorant*.

Fish knew he had to exercise since he spent so much time at his computer. He worked out three days a week. He ate a healthful diet. He drank plenty of water and got lots of sleep.

Tyler Blevins

Tyler "Ninja" Blevins is a pro esports player and streamer. Blevins was born June 5, 1991. He grew up in Grayslake, Illinois. His father passed his love of video games on to Blevins. For each hour Blevins played outside, his father allowed him one hour of video game time.

Tyler "Ninja" Blevins is one of the most famous streamers in the world.

Blevins often donates his winnings to charity.

Blevins started competing as a pro in 2009. He has played *Fortnite* and other games. Blevins helped the esports team Luminosity Gaming win the Gamescom PUBG Invitational Squads event in 2017. Blevins joined DJ Marshmello to play in the Fortnite Celebrity Pro-Am tournament in 2018. They won $1 million for charity.

Blevins practices with warm-ups and scrimmages. He reviews his old games. He says esports pros need more than good equipment. According to Blevins, communication is important for every esports team. Blevins is a popular streamer on Twitch and YouTube. He also represents many companies and helps them sell their products. He dreams of becoming a voice actor for animated characters.

Mike Begum

Mike "Brolylegs" Begum is a pro *Street Fighter* player. Begum uses his mouth and cheek to run his controller instead of his hands. He paired up with Jonathan Bautista in 2019 to win the Street Fighter League. They won a $10,000 prize!

Begum was born April 26, 1988. He was raised in Brownsville, Texas. He couldn't play physical sports, so his dad taught him to play video games. Begum played and practiced video games with his brother. They competed in *Super Smash Bros.* tournaments together.

Begum still practices *Street Fighter* for hours at a time. He works hard to perfect his skills. He streams games on Twitch and YouTube. He also coaches other players.

Mike "Brolylegs" Begum plays *Street Fighter* alongside his brother.

WOMEN IN ESPORTS

Women sometimes face discrimination in gaming. But as more women take home prizes in competitions, they encourage other talented women to compete in esports.

Melanie "meL" Capone competes alongside her team, Cloud9 White.

CHAPTER 3
COLLEGE ESPORTS PLAYERS

JUST LIKE PHYSICAL SPORTS, ESPORTS HAVE COLLEGE LEAGUES. In 2016, the University of California, Irvine (UCI), became the first public university in the US to start an official esports team. The school now has *League of Legends*, *Valorant*, and *Overwatch* teams.

UCI has a 3,500 square foot (325 sq. m) arena with 36 computers and other gaming equipment. UCI also offers esports scholarships. The school has an esports coach and physical and mental health specialists to keep players healthy. Over 170 colleges in the US have varsity esports teams.

UCI students compete in an *Overwatch 2* tournament.

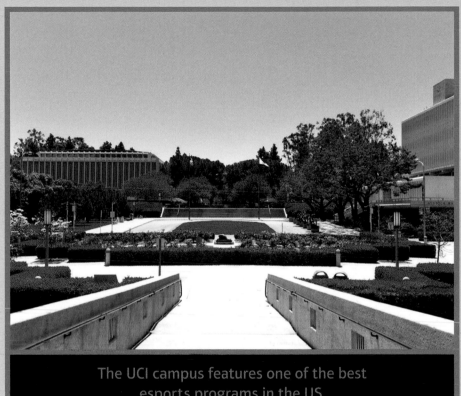
The UCI campus features one of the best esports programs in the US.

Victoria Winn

Victoria "Saffrona" Winn attended UCI. She played on the school's *Overwatch* team. Winn started console gaming with her dad and brothers when she was young.

During high school in Temecula, California, Winn began playing *Overwatch*. She was drawn to the game's strong female characters. Winn would finish her homework at

UCI esports players compete in an arena on campus.

school and rush home to play the game. She even founded an esports club at her high school.

At UCI, Winn and her teammates practiced against one another and with other teams. Winn says that it is important for teammates to communicate well with one another. Winn and the team watched videos of their old games to learn from past mistakes. The team played in tournaments against other colleges on the weekends.

Winn studied computer game science. She has worked as an intern at Riot Games. She wants to develop new games in the future.

Riot Games has developed popular games such as *League of Legends* and *Valorant*.

A college team prepares to compete in an esports event.

Ryann Baker

Ryann Baker is an esports player at Stephens College in Columbia, Missouri. She plays *Overwatch* on the varsity team at the all-women's college. Baker loves competing in esports.

As a kid, Baker first played video games on a Gameboy Color. She also began competing in horse jumping when she was six years old. In both sports, she likes competing with herself to improve her skills. Baker dreams of becoming a pro horse trainer and riding teacher. She also wants to stay active in the gaming community.

AN ALL-FEMALE COLLEGE TEAM

The Stephens College Stars are helping pave the way for women in college esports. It is the first college all-female varsity esports team. The Stars began competing in *Overwatch* championships in 2017.

Esports superstars come from many different backgrounds. But they all share a passion for gaming. Do you enjoy video games and competing against others? With a lot of practice, you could be the next esports superstar.

GLOSSARY

AMATEUR: taking part in an activity for fun, not to earn money

ARENA: an enclosed area used for public events

CONSOLE: a special computer that connects to a display (such as a TV) and is used to play video games

DEVELOP: to create or produce, especially over time

DISCRIMINATION: treating some people better or worse than others without any fair or proper reason

PRO: short for *professional*, taking part in an activity to earn money

SCHOLARSHIP: money given to a student to help pay for school

SCRIMMAGE: a practice game between two teams

STREAM: to broadcast or watch live video

VARSITY: the top team at a school

LEARN MORE

Electronic Sports Facts for Kids
https://kids.kiddle.co/Electronic_sports

Gardiner, Nora. *Tyler "Ninja" Blevins*. New York: Enslow, 2022.

How Professional Gaming Works
https://money.howstuffworks.com/professional-gaming.htm

Nicks, Erin. *Esports Stars*. Minneapolis: Abdo, 2021.

Schwartz, Heather E. *Esports Championships*. Minneapolis: Lerner Publications, 2024.

Video Game Facts for Kids
https://kids.kiddle.co/Video_games

INDEX

PHOTO ACKNOWLEDGEMENTS

Image credits: JOHANNES EISELE/AFP/Getty Images, p. 4; Adela Sznajder/Riot Games Inc/Getty Images, p. 6; Gerald Matzka/picture alliance/Getty Images, p. 7; Hara Amoros/Riot Games/Getty Images, p. 8; SMichal Konkol/Riot Games Inc./Getty Images, p. 9; Edwin Tan/Getty Images, p. 10; Jimmy Tudeschi/Shutterstock, p. 11; Joi Ito from Inbamura, Japan/Wikimedia Commons (CC 2.0), p. 12; Michal Konkol/Riot Games Inc./Getty Images, p. 13; Steven Ryan/Getty Images, p. 14; Kevork Djansezian/Getty Images, p. 15; Veja/Shutterstock, p. 16; Lance Skundrich/Riot Games Inc./Getty Images, p. 17; Robert Reiners/Getty Images, p. 18; Diego Donamaria/Getty Images, p. 19; AP Photo/The Monitor, Joel Martinez, p. 21; Adela Sznajder/Riot Games/Getty Images, p. 22; Allen J. Schaben/Los Angeles Times/Getty Images, pp. 23, 24, 26; Steve Cukrov/Shutterstock, p. 25; Piotr Swat/Shutterstock, p. 27; Ben Hasty/MediaNews Group/Reading Eagle/Getty Images, p. 28; RG-vc/Shutterstock, p. 29.
Cover: AP Photo/Christoph Soeder/picture-alliance/dpa; REUTERS/Thomas Peter/Alamy Stock Photo.